THE LITTLE BOOK OF

MINDFULNESS

First published in 2025 by OH
An Imprint of HEADLINE PUBLISHING GROUP LIMITED

1

Disclaimer:

Cataloguing in Publication Data is available from the British Library

ISBN 978-1-03542-298-2

Compiled and written by: Saneaah Muhammad
Editorial: Victoria Denne
Designed and typeset in Dosis by: Stephen Cary
Project manager: Russell Porter
Production: Rachel Burgess
Printed and bound in Dubai

HEADLINE PUBLISHING GROUP LIMITED
An Hachette UK Company
Carmelite House, 50 Victoria Embankment, London EC4Y 0DZ

The authorised representative in the EEA is Hachette Ireland, 8 Castlecourt Centre,
Dublin 15, D15 XTP3, Ireland (email: info@hbgi.ie)

www.headline.co.uk   www.hachette.co.uk

THE LITTLE BOOK OF

MINDFULNESS

FOR WHEN LIFE
GETS A LITTLE TOUGH

CONTENTS

INTRODUCTION – 6

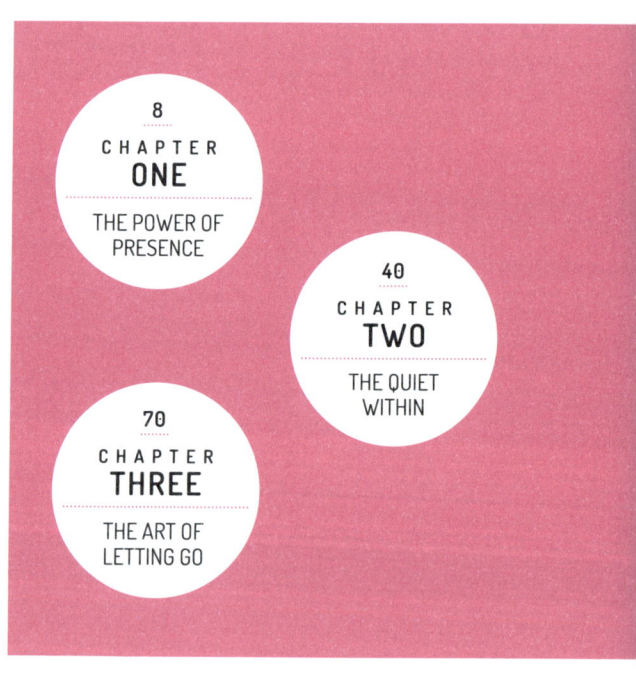

8
CHAPTER
ONE
THE POWER OF
PRESENCE

40
CHAPTER
TWO
THE QUIET
WITHIN

70
CHAPTER
THREE
THE ART OF
LETTING GO

104

C H A P T E R
FOUR

GRATITUDE IN
EVERY MOMENT

132

C H A P T E R
FIVE

SAVOURING
THE ORDINARY

162

C H A P T E R
SIX

MINDFULNESS AS
A WAY OF LIFE

INTRODUCTION

In a world that constantly pulls us in countless directions, mindfulness offers a peaceful refuge – a chance to pause, breathe and reconnect with the present moment. Amid the chaos of daily life, it can be easy to lose touch with the here and now, caught up in the rush of past regrets or future worries. But mindfulness encourages us to be fully present, to tune into the richness of each moment and to engage with life more deeply.

Mindfulness isn't about emptying the mind or escaping from life; rather, it's about filling our awareness with appreciation for what is unfolding right before us. It's the art of noticing, of being deeply attuned to our thoughts, feelings and surroundings without judgement or distraction. By cultivating mindfulness, we unlock a profound sense of clarity and calm that helps us navigate life with greater intention and purpose.

This little book offers a collection of wisdom from diverse voices, exploring the practice and true meaning of mindfulness. Each chapter delves into a different aspect of mindfulness, from the power of presence and the quiet within, to the art of letting go and savoring life's ordinary moments. Whether you're new to mindfulness or looking to deepen your practice, these insights will guide you toward greater awareness and well-being. Embrace the journey of living mindfully and discover how this simple yet transformative practice can help you find peace, clarity and joy in every moment.

CHAPTER
1

THE POWER OF PRESENCE

The present moment is the essence of mindfulness. It is where life truly happens, free from the burdens of the past and the anxieties of the future and instead being fully aware of the here and now. By embracing the "now" we open ourselves to clarity and tranquility, and fully experiencing the present allows us to live with intention and purpose, creating a deeper connection to ourselves and the world around us. As you journey through these quotes, embrace this moment fully – it's all we ever truly have.

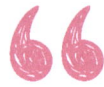

The past is a ghost, the future
a dream. All we ever have is now.

Eckhart Tolle

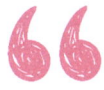

Do not dwell in the past, do not
dream of the future, concentrate
the mind on the present moment.

Buddha

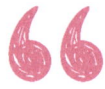

Forever is composed of nows.

Emily Dickinson

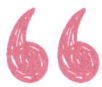

In mindfulness, we are not judging the present, we are simply noticing it.

Tara Brach

The more you practice being present, the more you'll feel the simplicity of life and the vastness of it at the same time.

Laura Vanderkam

You must live in the present, launch
yourself on every wave, find your
eternity in each moment.

Henry David Thoreau

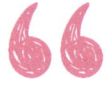

Nothing is worth
more than this day.

Johann Wolfgang von Goethe

The secret of health for both mind and body is not to mourn for the past, worry about the future, or anticipate troubles, but to live in the present moment wisely and earnestly.

Swami Sivananda

Do every act of your life as though it were the very last act of your life.

Marcus Aurelius

True presence in life is not found
in the things we do, but in how we
experience them.

Sadhguru

Be happy in the moment,
that's enough. Each moment is
all we need, not more.

Mother Teresa

The ability to be in the present
moment is a major component
of mental wellness.

Abraham Maslow

If you want to conquer the
anxiety of life, live in the moment,
live in the breath.

Amit Ray

It is only in the present
that life is truly lived.

Gabriel García Márquez

True happiness is... to enjoy the present, without anxious dependence upon the future.

Seneca

We are always getting ready
to live, but never living.

Ralph Waldo Emerson

The present moment is filled
with joy and happiness. If you are
attentive, you will see it.

Thích Nhất Hạnh

When you are present, everything
shifts. It becomes effortless.

Eckhart Tolle

The first step to presence
is a deep breath. From there,
the rest of life follows.

Sarah Blondin

Don't wait.
The time will never be just right.

Napoleon Hill

To be mindful is to embrace the present moment without resistance.

Anonymous

Mindfulness is the aware, balanced acceptance of the present experience.

Sylvia Boorstein

The only way to live is by accepting each minute as an unrepeatable miracle.

Tara Brach

Living mindfully means choosing to engage with life's moments without rushing through them.

Chade-Meng Tan

Yesterday is gone.
Tomorrow has not yet come.
We have only today.
Let us begin.

Mother Teresa

Happiness, not in another place but this place... not for another hour, but this hour.

Walt Whitman

A wise man is content with his lot, whatever it may be, without wishing for what he has not.

Seneca

Presence is the unlocking the
doors of your heart and mind.

Unknown

Living in the moment means letting go of the past and not waiting for the future. It means living your life consciously, aware that each moment you breathe is a gift.

Oprah Winfrey

The greatest gift you can give
someone is your presence.

Thích Nhất Hạnh

CHAPTER
2

THE QUIET WITHIN

Amidst the noise of everyday life, the quiet within offers a refuge of calm. Through mindfulness, we can learn to still the mind, allowing us to reconnect with our inner peace. In these moments of silence, we discover a deeper sense of clarity, presence and tranquility – an essential practice for navigating life's chaos with grace.

What lies behind us and what lies ahead of us are tiny matters compared to what lies within us.

Ralph Waldo Emerson

Breathe deeply.
You are alive in this moment.

Thích Nhất Hạnh

Between stimulus and
response, there is a space.
In that space is our power to
choose our response.

Viktor Frankl

If you are wholly perplexed
and in straits, have patience, for
patience is the key to joy.

Rumi

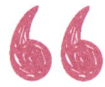

When you are present, you can
allow the mind to be as it is without
getting entangled.

Eckhart Tolle

When we accept what is, it
takes away its power over us.

Pema Chödrön

Be curious, not judgmental.

Walt Whitman

Non-judgement quiets the internal dialogue, and this opens once again the doorway to creativity.

Thomas Aquinas

Feelings are just visitors.
Let them come and go.

Mooji

Observe your thoughts,
don't believe them.

Byron Katie

You don't have to control your thoughts. You just have to stop letting them control you.

Dan Millman

Mindfulness means being awake.
It means knowing what you are doing.

Jon Kabat-Zinn

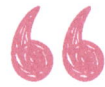

Awareness is all about restoring your freedom to choose what you want instead of what your past imposes on you.

Deepak Chopra

The more light you allow within you, the brighter the world you live in will be.

Shakti Gawain

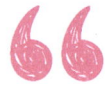

The greatest weapon against
stress is our ability to choose
one thought over another.

William James

Awareness is the greatest
agent for change.

Eckhart Tolle

Quiet the mind, and the
soul will speak.

Ma Jaya Sati Bhagavati

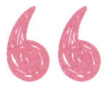

Do not be angry with the rain;
it simply does not know how
to fall upwards.

Vladimir Nabokov

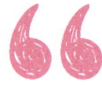

To be mindful is to give your full attention
to the moment you are in.

Dr. Shauna Shapiro

Being fully engaged with life brings us an inner calm and a sense of fulfillment.

Jon Kabat-Zinn

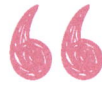

To the mind that is still, the whole universe surrenders.

Zhuangzi

The practice of mindfulness
brings the mind into harmony
with the body.

Jon Kabat-Zinn

Stillness is not about focusing
on nothingness; it's about creating
an emotional clearing to feel,
think and dream.

Brené Brown

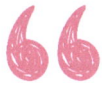

The greatest revelation is stillness.

Lao Tzu

The space between your thoughts
is where you find peace.

Wayne Dyer

The quieter you become,
the more you can hear.

Ram Dass

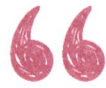

The beauty of mindfulness is that it helps you see life in its entirety without rushing to the next thing.

Carol Shields

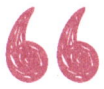

True peace comes from within.

Buddha

CHAPTER
3

THE ART OF LETTING GO

Change is the rhythm of life, a constant force that calls us to grow and evolve. Embracing it requires mindfulness – the ability to stay present and open amidst uncertainty. Letting go of grudges, fears and expectations is an act of liberation, freeing us from the weight of the past and allowing us to live with greater lightness and freedom. Mindfulness teaches us to release what no longer serves us, making room for new possibilities.

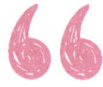

Life is a series of natural and spontaneous changes. Don't resist them; that only creates sorrow. Let reality be reality. Let things flow naturally forward in whatever way they like.

Lao Tzu

The only way to make sense out
of change is to plunge into it, move
with it, and join the dance.

Alan Watts

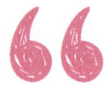

Change is the law of life.
And those who look only to the
past or present are certain to
miss the future.

John F. Kennedy

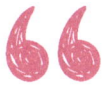

You cannot step twice into the same river, for other waters are continually flowing in.

Heraclitus

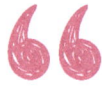

The measure of intelligence
is the ability to change.

Albert Einstein

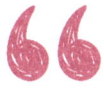

Your life does not get better by chance,
it gets better by change.

Jim Rohn

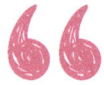

Progress is impossible without change, and those who cannot change their minds cannot change anything.

George Bernard Shaw

Courage is the power to let
go of the familiar.

Raymond Lindquist

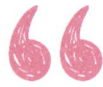

When we are no longer able to change a situation, we are challenged to change ourselves.

Viktor Frankl

Change your thoughts and
you change your world.

Norman Vincent Peale

Our anxiety does not come
from thinking about the future,
but from wanting to control it.

Kahlil Gibran

Whatever the present moment
contains, accept it as if you had chosen it.
Always work with it, not against it.

Eckhart Tolle

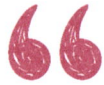

A tree that is unbending is easily broken. The hard and stiff will be broken. The soft and supple will prevail.

Lao Tzu

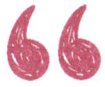

To exist is to change, to change
is to mature, to mature is to go
on creating oneself endlessly.

Henri Bergson

The present changes the past.
Looking back, you do not find what
you left behind.

Kiran Desai

The only way to transform your life is to be aware of it moment by moment.

Unknown

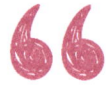

You can only lose what you cling to.

Buddha

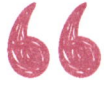

Letting go gives us freedom,
and freedom is the only condition
for happiness.

Thích Nhất Hạnh

Some of us think holding on makes us strong, but sometimes it is letting go.

Hermann Hesse

When I let go of what I am,
I become what I might be.

Lao Tzu

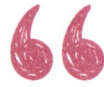

The moment you let go, you create
space for something better.

Eckhart Tolle

Detachment is not that you should own nothing, but that nothing should own you.

Ali ibn Abi Talib

The act of letting go is an
act of acceptance.

Jack Kornfield

When you release expectations,
you are free to enjoy things for what
they are, instead of what you think
they should be.

Mandy Hale

Letting go is the key to happiness.

Buddha

Surrender to what is. Let go of what was.
Have faith in what will be.

Sonia Ricotti

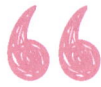

It is not the daily increase but the daily decrease. Hack away at the unessential.

Bruce Lee

Let go or be dragged.

Zen proverb

Change is the only constant in life.
Embrace it with mindfulness.

Heraclitus

In the process of letting go,
we discover who we really are.

Anonymous

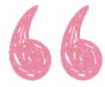

When you let go, you create space
for new possibilities to enter.

Anonymous

When you stop searching for
answers and just live the question,
life becomes its own answer.

Rainer Maria Rilke

CHAPTER

4

GRATITUDE IN EVERY MOMENT

Gratitude is the heart of mindfulness, transforming ordinary moments into precious blessings. By focusing on what we have, rather than what we lack, we invite joy and contentment into the present. It shifts our perspective, allowing us to recognize the abundance that surrounds us. These words of wisdom celebrate the power of gratitude, offering wisdom to help cultivate a deeper appreciation for life in every moment.

Gratitude turns what we
have into enough.

Aesop

When you are grateful, fear disappears and abundance appears.

Tony Robbins

Acknowledging the good that
you already have in your life is the
foundation for all abundance.

Eckhart Tolle

Gratitude is not only the greatest of
virtues but the parent of all others.

Cicero

Let us rise up and be thankful,
for if we didn't learn a lot today,
at least we learned a little.

Buddha

Mindfulness and gratitude go hand in hand; one reveals the beauty of the present, and the other celebrates it.

Unknown

Walk as if you are kissing the
Earth with your feet.

Thích Nhất Hạnh

Gratitude is when memory is stored
in the heart and not in the mind.

Lionel Hampton

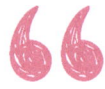

Mindfulness isn't difficult;
we just need to remember to do it.

Sharon Salzberg

Gratitude is the practice
of opening your heart to the
present moment.

Unknown

When you arise in the morning,
think of what a privilege it is to be alive,
to think, to enjoy, to love.

Marcus Aurelius

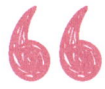

Gratitude bestows reverence,
allowing us to encounter everyday
epiphanies, those transcendent moments
of awe that change forever how we
experience life and the world.

John Milton

Gratitude unlocks the fullness of life.
It turns denial into acceptance, chaos into
order, confusion into clarity.

Melody Beattie

The miracle is not to walk on water.
The miracle is to walk on the green Earth,
dwelling deeply in the present moment
and feeling truly alive.

Thích Nhất Hạnh

Mindfulness is simply being aware of what is happening right now without wishing it were different; enjoying the pleasant without holding on when it changes (which it will); being with the unpleasant without fearing it will always be this way (which it won't).

James Baraz

It is through gratitude for the present moment that the spiritual dimension of life opens up.

Eckhart Tolle

Life is a dance. Mindfulness is witnessing that dance.

Amit Ray

When you realize nothing is lacking,
the whole world belongs to you.

Lao Tzu

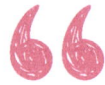

The little things?
The little moments?
They aren't little.

Jon Kabat-Zinn

Drink your tea slowly and reverently,
as if it is the axis on which the world earth
revolves – slowly, evenly, without
rushing toward the future.

Thích Nhất Hạnh

Cultivate the habit of being grateful for every good thing that comes to you, and to give thanks continuously.

Ralph Waldo Emerson

Gratitude is the fairest blossom
which springs from the soul.

Henry Ward Beecher

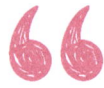

Wear gratitude like a cloak and it will feed every corner of your life.

Rumi

The real gift of gratitude is that
the more grateful you are, the more
present you become.

Robert Holden

In ordinary life, we hardly realize that we receive a great deal more than we give, and that it is only with gratitude that life becomes rich.

Dietrich Bonhoeffer

Don't ruin today with the regrets of yesterday.

John Dryden

CHAPTER
5

SAVOURING THE ORDINARY

Life's most beautiful moments often reside in the ordinary: a warm cup of coffee, a quiet walk, the rustle of leaves. By slowing down and paying attention, we can savour these fleeting wonders. Mindfulness invites us to embrace the simple joys that surround us every day, reminding us that there is beauty in the mundane and peace in the present moment.

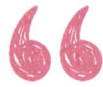

When you're mindful, your whole life becomes a meditation.

Pema Chödrön

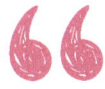

Savour the moments that
can't be captured.

Anonymous

Enjoy the little things, for one day you may look back and realize they were the big things.

Robert Brault

Every moment is a fresh beginning.

T. S. Eliot

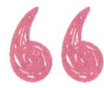

Sometimes, the simple things
are the most profound.

Anonymous

Be happy for this moment.
This moment is your life.

Omar Khayyam

The ordinary acts we practice every day at home are of more importance to the soul than their simplicity might suggest.

Thomas Moore

Life is what happens when
you're busy making other plans.

John Lennon

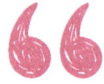

Rejoice in the things that are present;
all else is beyond thee.

Michel de Montaigne

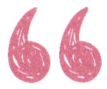

As you walk and eat and travel,
be where you are. Otherwise, you
will miss most of your life.

Buddha

Keep your love of nature, for that
is the true way to understand art
more and more.

Vincent Van Gogh

Be where your feet are.

Anonymous

Happiness is not something
ready-made. It comes from
your own actions.

Dalai Lama

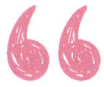

To live is so startling, it leaves little
time for anything else.

Emily Dickinson

The day is always his who works with
serenity and great aims.

Ralph Waldo Emerson

In the sweetness of friendship let
there be laughter, for in the dew of little
things the heart finds its morning
and is refreshed.

Khalil Gibran

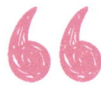

The simple things are also the
most extraordinary things, and only
the wise can see them.

Paulo Coelho

Simplicity is the ultimate sophistication.

Leonardo da Vinci

Every flower blooms at its own pace.

Suzy Kassem

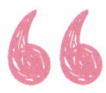

Nothing is more precious than
being in the present moment.
Fully alive, fully aware.

Thích Nhất Hạnh

Find ecstasy in life;
the mere sense of living
is joy enough.

Emily Dickinson

Do not despise the small joys of life, for they make the heart rich and the soul full.

Anonymous

Beauty in things exists in the mind
which contemplates them.

David Hume

Let the beauty of what you
love be what you do.

Rumi

In every walk with nature,
one receives far more than he seeks.

John Muir

The more you praise and
celebrate your life, the more there
is in life to celebrate.

Oprah Winfrey

If you can't find beauty in the small things, you'll never find it at all.

Anonymous

Life is really simple, but we insist on making it complicated.

Confucius

CHAPTER

6

MINDFULNESS AS A WAY OF LIFE

Mindfulness is not a fleeting practice but a way of living – an enduring commitment to being fully alive in each moment.
By bringing mindfulness into every aspect of your daily existence, you begin to live with a heightened sense of awareness, intention and purpose. It's about creating a rhythm of presence that guides you through all the moments of your life, whether mundane or extraordinary.

Mindfulness is a way of befriending ourselves and our experience.

Jon Kabat-Zinn

The mind is everything.
What you think, you become.

Buddha

Every breath we take, every step
we make, can be filled with peace,
joy and serenity.

Thích Nhất Hạnh

Mindfulness isn't just about breathing. It's about cultivating presence in every action.

Dr. Daniel Goleman

You must learn a new way to think before
you can master a new way to be.

Marianne Williamson

Mindfulness is not a technique or a
tool to be used, it is a way of life.

Jon Kabat-Zinn

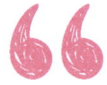

The present moment is all you
have to work with.

Pema Chödrön

Mindfulness gives you time. Time gives you choices. Choices, skillfully made, lead to freedom.

Bhante H. Gunaratana

When you live in the moment,
life is full of wonder.

Jack Kornfield

Mindfulness is the ability to keep
your awareness open and alive,
to the present moment.

Chögyam Trungpa

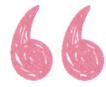

The only thing that's permanent is change, and mindfulness helps us navigate it with grace.

Richard Davidson

Living mindfully means focusing
on the small moments as much as
the big ones.

Adyashanti

Mindfulness is the art of paying attention on purpose in the present moment, without judgement.

Jon Kabat-Zinn

Mindfulness is the conscious practice
of being present in our lives.

Daniel J. Siegel

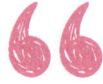

The quality of your life is determined by the quality of your thoughts.

Marcus Aurelius

The simple act of paying attention
can bring profound peace.

Thích Nhất Hạnh

You are today where your thoughts have brought you; you will be tomorrow where your thoughts take you.

James Allen

To understand the world, one must
first understand oneself.

Confucius

Mindfulness is the practice of choosing to be aware, regardless of what life is presenting.

Trudy Goodman

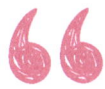

When we practice mindfulness,
we are able to truly experience the
richness of our own lives.

Marsha Linehan

Life is a mirror, and it will reflect back
to the thinker what he thinks into it.

Ernest Holmes

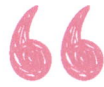

Mindfulness is a way of feeling alive in the present, understanding that we are part of the world, not separate from it.

Maya Angelou

Awakening is not about learning
anything new. It's about remembering
that which we have forgotten.

Adyashanti

When you practice mindfulness,
you create a space where peace
can blossom.

Jon Kabat-Zinn

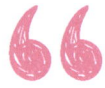

The more we step into each moment
without judgement, the more life
flows in its natural rhythm.

Byron Katie

When you are grounded in the present, life flows with a deep sense of ease.

Jack Kornfield

The secret to happiness is not in doing
more but in being more aware of
what is already here.

Dr. Wayne Dyer

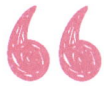

The beauty of life is revealed in the way we pay attention to it.

Oprah Winfrey

We are what we think.
All that we are arises with our
thoughts. With our thoughts,
we make the world.

Buddha